A smart confectioner's in 1818 with displays of cakes, biscuits, tarts, syllabubs and glass jars containing flavoured jellies.

SWEETS AND SWEET SHOPS

Laura Mason

Shire Publications

Contents

British Library Cataloguing in Publication Data: Mason, Laura. Sweets and sweet shops. – (Shire album; no. 344) 1. Confectionery – Great Britain – History I. Title 380.1'45'641853'0941. ISBN 0 7478 0424 9.

ACKNOWLEDGEMENTS

The author would like to thank the following people for their help with this book: Mr I. Day; Mr A. Millward; Mrs O. Shipperbottom and the late R. Shipperbottom; Mr R. Weir; the staff of the Borthwick Institute, University of York; York Castle Museum; Mr T. Chadwick, at Joseph Dobson & Sons, Elland; Mr L. Murray, at Maxilin Ltd, Bolton; Mr D. Little and Mrs S. Torr, at Trebor-Bassett (formerly M. A. Craven), York; Mrs G. Wells, Trebor Basset Ltd; Mrs S. Foden and the library staff at Cadbury Schweppes Ltd; Mr M. Grimes and Mr J. Matchett at Terry's-Suchard, York; the staff at the Photographic Library, Beamish, the North of England Open Air Museum; Examiner News and Information Services, Huddersfield; Julie Ann Lambert at the Bodleian Library, Oxford.

Illustrations are reproduced by kind permission of the following: Beamish, the North of England Open Air Museum, pages 4, 17 (both), 19 (top), 20 (top), 25 (top), 30 (both); Bodleian Library, University of Oxford: John Johnson Collection, Trade Cards 11, page 6 (top); Bodleian Library, University of Oxford, Trade Cards 7 (63), page 13 (bottom); Ivan Day, page 7 (top); Joseph Dobson & Sons, Elland, page 14; *The Huddersfield Daily Examiner*, pages 13 (top), 21 (bottom); Imperial War Museum, page 29 (bottom); Maxilin Ltd, Bolton, page 28 (top left); Nestlé S. A., pages 16 (top), 24; Mrs O. Shipperbottom, page 11 (top); Terry's-Suchard, York; the staff at the Bottom); Trebor Bassett Ltd, pages 11 (bottom), 20 (bottom), 22 (bottom), 25 (bottom), 27 (both), 28 (top right), 31; Robin Weir, page 8 (bottom); Wrigley's Ltd, page 29 (top); York Castle Museum, cover; City of York Libraries, page 12. The illustration on page 15 (bottom) is as shown in *Package and Print* by Alec Davies (1967), and that on page 18 is from the *Illustrated London News*.

All other illustrations are from the author's collection. Their sources are as follows: *Culpeper's Herbal*, 1817, page 5 (top); *Dandies sans-sis-sous* by Charles Williams, 1818, page 1; *The Italian Confectioner* by G. A. Jarrin, 1820, page 6 (bottom); *Le Confiseur Royal* by Mme Utrecht-Friedel, 1818, page 9; *The Modern Baker* by John Kirkland, 1931, page 10; Skuse's *Confectioner's Handbook*, c.1890, page 23; Skuse's *Complete Confectioner*, c.1900, pages 7 (bottom), 16 (bottom), 19 (bottom), 21 (top), 26 (top); Thomas Mills & Brother catalogue, 1930, pages 3 (both), 5 (bottom), 15 (top), 28 (bottom).

Cover illustration: *Terry's shop, York Castle Museum.*

Published in 1999 by Shire Publications Ltd, Cromwell House, Church Street, Princes Risborough, Buckinghamshire HP27 9AA, UK. (Website: www.shirebooks.co.uk)

Copyright © 1999 by Laura Mason. First published 1999. Shire Album 344. ISBN 0 7478 0424 9.

Laura Mason is hereby identified as the author of this work in accordance with Section 77 of the Copyright, Designs and Patents Act 1988.

Printed in Great Britain by CIT Printing Services Ltd, Press Buildings, Merlins Bridge, Haverfordwest, Pembrokeshire SA61 1XF.

The art and craft of confectionery

Vibrantly colourful sweets in jars on the shelf reflect centuries of trial and error in sugar boiling. This is the general name for the craft of working with syrup. At the start of the nineteenth century confectioners worked by taking samples of boiling syrup, dropping them into cold water and manipulating them between their fingers. This showed the *degree* or *stage* that the syrup had reached. Particular stages are necessary for particular sweets.

Elaborate ornamental jars for confectionery sold by Thomas Mills & Brother, Philadelphia, USA, in 1930.

Sugar boiling exploits the relationship between the sugar concentration in syrup and the temperature at which it boils. The more sugar, the higher the temperature will be. Continued boiling leads to more water evaporating. As the concentration of sugar in the syrup increases, so the temperature rises. Eventually, only molten sugar remains.

A sugar-boiling thermometer, calibrated in degrees Fahrenheit (Thomas Mills & Brother). Some basic stages recognised by confectioners and associated temperatures are: thread (230°F, 110°C); soft ball (240°F, 115°C); hard ball (260°F, 127°C); crack (280°F, 138°C); hard crack (300°F, 149°C). At 309°F (154°C), sugar burns.

Sweet shops have always been attractive to small children. This one is from the 1930s.

Graining the sugar (re-crystallising syrup to make candy) is also important. By 1750 French confectioners observed that syrup containing lemon juice was *greasy*, that is, it did not grain easily. They exploited this to make clear, hard confections. In Britain, confectioners referred to lemon juice as a *doctor*. Tartaric acid (from grapes) was discovered to have a similar action. Glucose syrup (first produced in the mid eighteenth century) was also found to act as a doctor.

Sugar in the kitchen cupboard is a crystalline form of a substance called sucrose, composed of two simpler sugars, fructose and glucose, bonded together. Doctors alter the relative proportions of fructose and glucose during boiling. They are vital to the manufacture of non-crystalline boiled sweets, such as sparkling clear fruit drops, barley sugar and confections of the seaside rock and humbug type. By 1840 confectioners knew that tartaric acid or cream of tartar made their job easier; by 1900, they were using glucose. These substances, now known as *interfering agents*, are essential to the confectionery industry.

Sweet traditions

The simple formula of sweet equals good obscures the history of confectionery. Sweets were formerly precious rarities and status symbols. Notions of this are still influential. They date back six hundred years to when sugar was an exotic, expensive luxury. It was used in medicine, celebrations and food preservation. By 1800, these diverse strands had aligned, culminating in something we would recognise as a sweet shop.

Sugar sweetened early medicinal *confections* and preserved herbal extracts. Liquorice, horehound drops and coltsfoot rock belong to this tradition. Alone or in candy with roses or violets, sugar was thought good for colds. Comfits (nuts or seeds covered in sugar) were considered to aid digestion in the late Middle Ages, just as mints are still offered after dinner today. Christmas and Easter novelties originated with ideas fashionable in the fifteenth century when confectioners moulded candy or marzipan figures. A century later, sugar was widely used for fruit preserving. Fruit and flowers candied against the scarcity of winter enhanced the luxury image of confectionery.

Horehound (right) and coltsfoot, two medicinal herbs still used in confectionery, as pictured in Culpeper's 'Herbal' in 1817.

The sugar 'bacon and eggs' of seaside rock shops and conversation lozenges have their roots in practices first recorded at the end of Queen Elizabeth I's reign. Wealthy ladies whiled away the hours with sugar work, sometimes composing entire 'banquets' of sweet foods. Under French influence, the sugar banquet evolved into the eighteenth-century *dessert*, an elegant collation of fresh and preserved fruit, delicate biscuits, creams and sugar work. *Sweetmeats*, their collective name, was abbreviated into *sweeties* or *sweets*. From then on, the story is one of falling prices and technical innovation. Sugar became a necessity, and sweets a commonplace part of childhood.

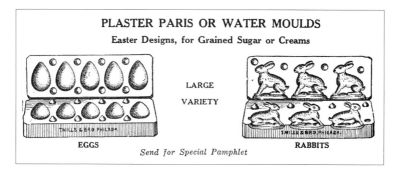

Plaster moulds sold by Thomas Mills & Brother, Philadelphia, USA. Sugar candy figures, popular for centuries, were replaced by chocolate novelties in Britain in the twentieth century.

The ingredients of sweets

Sugar cane and sugar refining were introduced to the Mediterranean region from the East after the Islamic conquest in the seventh century AD. Sugar gradually spread west, crossing the Atlantic with sixteenth-century explorers. By 1800 it was grown on a large scale in the Caribbean islands. Sugar beet was developed as a crop in France during the Napoleonic Wars: originally it was intended to provide an alternative to Caribbean sugar, supplies of which were affected by a British blockade. By the end of the nineteenth century sugar beet was grown in many European countries.

Initially, sparkling white candy in loaves was the best grade available, but confectioners worked mostly with impure brown sugar. It was clarified to produce a clear, colourless syrup. When modern refining techniques developed in the mid nineteenth century, confectioners could buy inexpensive refined crystal sugar.

Confectionery ingredients known for millennia include almonds, pistachios and many fruits. The Romans traded cinnamon, cloves and ginger, as did the Moslems,

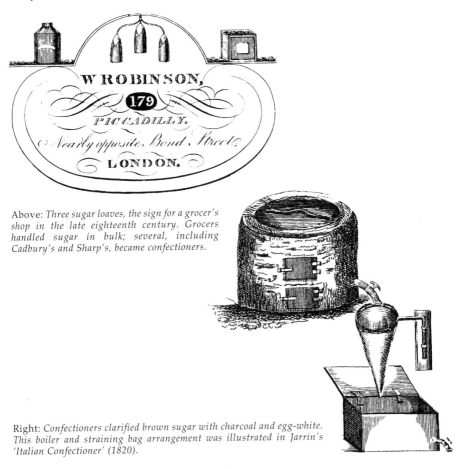

Above: *Three sugar loaves, the sign for a grocer's shop in the late eighteenth century. Grocers handled sugar in bulk; several, including Cadbury's and Sharp's, became confectioners.*

Right: *Confectioners clarified brown sugar with charcoal and egg-white. This boiler and straining bag arrangement was illustrated in Jarrin's 'Italian Confectioner' (1820).*

6

until fifteenth-century explorers opened alternative routes to the Indies. Orange and lemon trees were introduced into Europe at the same time as sugar. Rose water, too, is of eastern origin. Liquorice, originally native to Central Asia, has been grown in Britain since the Dark Ages. Tradition states that it was grown at Pontefract in Yorkshire by medieval monks, but available records mention cultivation there only from the mid seventeenth century.

The discovery of the Americas introduced chocolate to the Old World; the cacao tree which provides the raw material is native to Central America. The first Europeans to describe it were Spanish conquistadors, soon after 1492. Vanilla and pineapples are also native to the Americas.

Gum arabic and tragacanth, essential in lozenges and fruit gums, are collected from trees in Turkey and North Africa. Gelatine, extracted from animal bones, was used from an early date, as was pectin from citrus fruits, quinces and apples. Milk, cream and butter have all been produced in Britain since prehistoric times, but vegetable fats important in confectionery, especially coconut oil and palm oil, have been imported only since the nineteenth century. Modified starches, used in many sweets, are modern products.

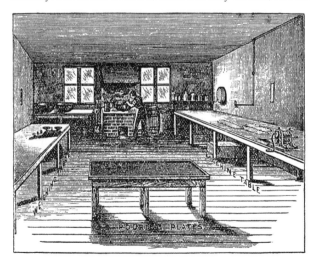

Little space or equipment was needed for a confectioner's, even around 1900, when this illustration was published in Skuse's 'Complete Confectioner'. Many companies began in such workrooms.

7

Terry's shopfront, York, c.1900. Terry's made sugar confectionery, chocolate, and ran a pastrycook's and a restaurant – a combination of trades typical of nineteenth-century confectioners.

The Georgian confectioner

Some confectionery companies can trace their origins to Georgian times. Joseph Fry was making chocolate in Bristol by 1761. About the same time, George Dunhill is said to have devised the liquorice Pontefract cake. Both men were apothecaries. So was Joseph Terry, who in 1828 joined a York confectioner's, Berry & Bayldon (established in 1767); they made sweets, lozenges, comfits and candied peel. Other confectionery companies began in other trades. In 1785 Mary Tuke established a grocer's business in York, which eventually developed into Rowntree's. Cadbury's began as tea and coffee dealers in Birmingham in 1824.

Books published by confectioners around 1800 show they dealt with many foods. In 1789 Frederick Nutt included numerous biscuit and ice cream recipes in his *Complete Confectioner*. Thirty years later, in *The Italian Confectioner*, G. A. Jarrin discussed fruit preserving and regretted that sugar sculptures had become unfashionable. In *The Confectioner's Oracle* (1830), William Gunter included savoury recipes. Confectioners were often pastrycooks as well. All these men were linked with a shop in Berkeley Square, London, established in 1769 by an Italian called Domenico Negri. Italian and French influence are a consistent theme in British confectionery.

William Gunter, 1830. Gunter's were famous for the excellence of their ices well into the twentieth century.

8

Panning comfits, an ancient confectionery technique, shown in 'Le Confiseur Royal' (Mme Utrecht-Friedel, 1818). The confectioner is using a balancing pan, like a huge copper saucer, suspended above a charcoal stove (which would not be as hot as the picture implies).

Fruit for preserving was important. Gunter's was supplied from its own gardens (commemorated in street names, including Gunter Grove, in Chelsea). Preserving involved gentle cooking and soaking in successively stronger syrups. Shape, colour and flavour were retained whilst the concentration of sugar increased. The fruit was stored in syrup or drained and candied. The process was not entirely reliable. If mould began to grow, the confectioner was instructed to re-boil the fruit. Fruit was also stored in brandy and made into jams, marmalades and pastes or dripped through flannel bags for limpid, pectin-set jellies.

Fresh and preserved fruits were used in creams and ices. These, made by chilling sealed containers of flavoured cream in ice and salt, were still novel. Fruit juice and sugar also went into syllabubs. A complete dessert could be ordered from a confectioner, who would also rent out frames and mirrors to put under the dishes for an elegant presentation.

Comfits (also known as sugarplums or *dragées*) were made by panning. Nuts or seeds, placed in a warm balancing pan, were rubbed with weak syrup so that thin layers of sugar built up around them. With each 'charge' of syrup, the comfits gradually increased in size. Caraway comfits, traditional favourites, went out of fashion in Britain, but sugar almonds remained popular. So did hundreds-and-thousands. Georgian confectioners knew these as *nonpareils* and dredged them over chocolate drops, creams and icing, as they were still scattered on buns for birthday teas in the 1950s.

9

Apothecaries and confectioners both used sugar paste. The formula, unchanged since the sixteenth century, included powdered sugar, gum tragacanth and water. It was flavoured with musk, ambergris, rose or violet for breath-sweetening lozenges. Floral cachous and Parma Violets are echoes of this idea. Liquorice, good for coughs, was also used, as was mint, for digestion. Another confection which crossed from pharmacy to sweets was marshmallow. Extract of mallow root, good for chest complaints but bitter, was replaced with apple juice, and the heavy mixture was lightened with beaten egg-white. Jujubes (chewy gum sweets) were also used for coughs.

Nut-based sweets were important. Pralines (burnt almonds) were made from almonds and caramelised sugar. Marzipan was popular and was often modelled to imitate fruits. Almond mixtures were also baked into elegant little biscuits. Jarrin's recipe for nougat in 1820 was almonds in caramel syrup, similar to *nougat noir* as still made in France. Small shops and street stalls called their version almond hardbake.

Confectioners made preparations of sugar to ornament fashionable desserts. These included *sands* of coloured sugar, and rock sugar made by adding hot syrup to royal icing, which foamed and set. Rock candy was made by growing sugar crystals on sticks in warm syrup. Many sweets were submerged in syrup for a few hours to crystallise them with a thin layer of sparkling sugar.

Drops were simply any suitable mixture dropped on to marble or oiled paper to set. Sugar melted with fruit juice, rose or orange-flower water, or water and

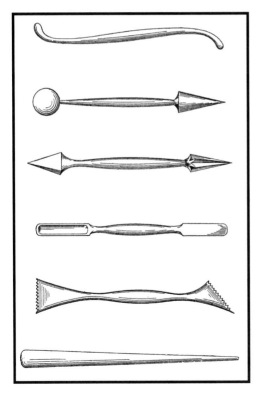

*Modelling tools for marzipan, as depicted in
'The Modern Baker' by John Kirkland (1931).*

10

peppermint oil were all used. These mixtures were also poured in sheets and cut into pieces when they candied. Some are still regional favourites: cough-candy in northern England, tablet (made from sugar and milk) in Scotland, and Kendal Mint Cake.

Barley sugar was originally made from sugar boiled with barley water to a high temperature. Whilst still hot, it was worked by 'pulling' over an iron hook fixed to the wall. The sugar was stretched over this, pulling and folding until it became white and shiny. By 1800 barley water was no longer used. Some confectioners began using syrup doctored with lemon juice instead. Poured on to a marble slab, the golden mixture was cut into sticks and twisted in spirals or deposited in drops, similar to modern barley sugar.

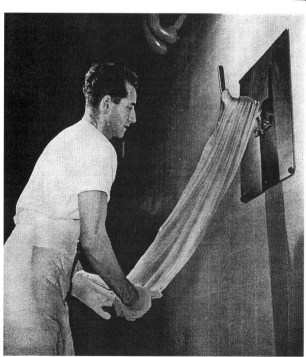

'Pulling' sugar is another ancient and enduring confectionery technique, essential for rock, humbugs and other striped sweets.

11

The Victorian sweet shop

The names of many sweets now considered traditional were first recorded between 1800 and 1850. In *The Table Book* (1827), William Hone described Twelfth Night (6th January) displays in pastrycooks' and confectioners' shops: 'upright cylinder show-glasses, containing pepper-mint drops, elecampane, sugar-sticks, hard-bake, brandy-balls, and bulls-eyes are carefully polished; their lolly-pops are fresh encased, and look as white as the stems of tobacco-pipes.' By this date, elecampane, originally a medicinal conserve of *Inula helenium*, was lemon-flavoured candy. The date when lolly-pop came to mean a sweet on a stick is unknown; 'lolly' means tongue in parts of northern England, and the term was probably just dialect for a sweet. Comparison to white (clay) pipe stems suggests sticks of pulled sugar.

A recipe from about 1830 for brandy-balls suggests these were similar to bullseyes or humbugs, small pieces of clear dark sugar striped with white. Such sweets were also called *pennets*, a name which hints at more ancient origins: it is a corruption, via medieval Latin, of Arabic *al-fanid*, which meant sugar worked until white. Another pulled sweet dated by tradition to the 1830s is Edinburgh rock. This uses a relatively low-boiled syrup, pulled and grained to give a crumbly texture.

Colourful names for sweets are nothing new. A recipe manuscript kept by confectioner William Finemore between *c.*1830 and *c.*1850 commemorates heroes, villains and battles from the Napoleonic wars in pulled sugar: Wellington sticks (red, blue and yellow), Nelson balls (red or yellow), Bonaparte's ribs (striped yellow or pink) and Gibraltar rock (a complex pattern of red and white sugar). The names, in use twenty years after the events, show both their national importance and the

6th January (Twelfth Night) was an important day of the Christmas season. The crowd are so busy admiring the confectioner's display that the urchins have pinned the clothes of two people together. (William Hone, 'The Table Book', 1827)

Striping a batch at Joseph Dobson & Sons, Elland, West Yorkshire, in 1949. Thin strips of white pulled sugar are arranged on top of clear boiled sugar. After this, the batch will be stretched out into a rope and cut into small sweets.

conservatism of confectioners and consumers.

S. W. Stavely, in a provincial publication called *The Whole New Art of Confectionary* [sic] (1830), told how to make plain twist (white pulled sugar) and paradise twist (streaked with clear red sugar) in the 1820s. In *London Labour and the London Poor* (*c*.1850), Sir Henry Mayhew recorded pulled sugar sticks with words in them: 'When snapped asunder, in any part, the stick presents a sort of coloured inscription.'

Sweet-tooth heaven – a mid-Victorian confectioner's shop lined with boxes and jars full of goodies.

13

This design for a sweet wrapper was printed for Joseph Dobson & Sons, Elland, West Yorkshire, in 1852, around the time that synthetic fruit flavours were first used.

Amongst others, Mayhew was shown 'Do you love me?' and 'Do you love sprats?' and was told such products were highly profitable. Mayhew described other sweets available from street stalls: hardbake, almond toffee, halfpenny lollipops, black balls, bullseyes and rose acid (a rose-flavoured version of the newly popular high-boiled sugar and tartaric acid *acid drop*). At adjacent stalls, one might buy sherbet – a cold, effervescent drink made with tartaric acid, bicarbonate of soda and water.

Toffee was first noted in the early nineteenth century. Everton toffee was sugar and butter cooked together to hard crack (149°C – see lower illustration on page 3), to make a crunchy sweet. According to tradition, it was sold by Molly Bushell in Everton (then a suburb of Liverpool); at least one maker appears to have been established there by 1812. Similar sweets became popular elsewhere. Doncaster butterscotch was made by Parkinson's, who began trading in 1817, and Farrah's Harrogate Toffee (still made) dates to 1840.

Food manufacturers generally were criticised at this time for using harmful ingredients. Confectioners favoured bright but toxic colours: copper-derived greens and blues, or harmful vegetable pigments such as gamboge. White sweets were bulked up with pipe-clay. When white arsenic was mistakenly used instead in Bradford in the 1850s, the resulting lozenges proved fatal to twenty people. Legislation was introduced to protect consumers. The expanding chemical industry eventually provided vibrant and relatively safe colours, as well as synthetic flavours. This gave impetus to the expanding sector of high-boiled sweets.

The Great Exhibition of 1851 was an opportunity for British confectioners to display their skill in sugar boiling, and the world was dazzled by their ingenuity with transparent confections. Numerous jewel-bright sweets were inspired by fruit preserving (a skill rapidly passing to canning companies). Pear drops, fruit drops, rhubarb and custard, sour cherries, pineapple cubes and, in Scotland, soor plums, survived long after the novelty had worn off. Technology also solved problems. The

Patterns for fruit drops were limited only by the designer's imagination and popular taste. These, from the catalogue of Thomas Mills & Brother in 1930, had probably been offered for decades previously.

new rail network carried heavy packages of sweets cheaply and swiftly; tins protected them from humidity and abrasion, and cheap printed colour labels enhanced packages.

Companies that are still household names were starting. Barker & Dobson began trading in 1834 in Liverpool, and Callard & Bowser in 1837 in Finchley. George Bassett founded his company around 1842 in Sheffield, and by 1848 Barratt's were established in London. Mary Ann Craven of York took over her deceased husband's business in 1862. Pascall's was founded near Oxford Street, London, in 1866. Clarnico was founded in 1872 and Needler's established in Hull in 1886. Scotland, too, had a flourishing confectionery industry, based on sugar imported to 'Sugaropolis' – the port of Greenock, a major refining centre. Small companies were scattered through Britain. Sweet shops were everywhere, from the poorest streets of tenements to the grandest thoroughfares.

In an age of uncertain healthcare, sugar paste lozenges were important. Producing them

The smart frontage of a pastrycook's and confectioner's shop depicted on a paper bag made by Robinson's of Bristol, c.1880. The drawing was probably from stock, customised for the business concerned.

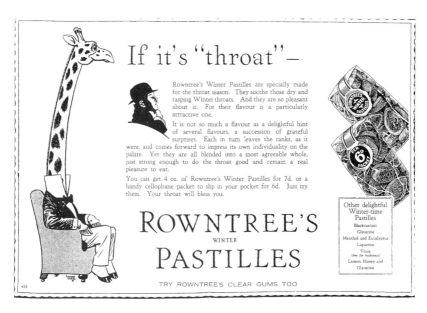

The link between sweets and medicine endures – an advertisement for throat pastilles made by Rowntree's in the 1930s.

by hand, so that each contained the same dose of therapeutic ingredients, was skilled work. LL&P stood for liquorice, linseed and paregoric, which contained opium, now illegal (as is chlorodyne, used in LL&C lozenges). In Lancashire, Thomas Fryer and Edward Smith MD devised Victory V gums and lozenges. James Lofthouse, a Fleetwood pharmacist, used sugar paste for lozenges containing his liquorice, capsicum, eucalyptus and menthol syrup (formulated in 1860) – the origin of Fisherman's Friends. Sugar paste was also extruded to make *pipe*; coltsfoot rock is a form of this. More entertaining were conversation lozenges stamped with mottoes. Solemn temperance maxims have not survived, but Love Hearts still make flippant and flirtatious statements.

Smooth fondant cream made from soft-ball syrup, grained when cool, became a favourite. Pure white, solid but with a melting texture, and simple to make, it began to replace candy. Flavoured with rose or violet, it recalled earlier traditions. Using the new idea of starch-moulding, it was formed into innumerable fantasy shapes. The children's favourite was the

Starch moulding by hand, as shown in Skuse's 'Complete Confectioner'. Left to right: smoothing starch in a tray; 'printing', using plaster moulds fixed to a wooden batten; filling the prints with syrup. Filled trays were placed in a heated drying room, where the starch drew moisture out of the confections so that they set.

Pulling out a 'string' of seaside rock from a batch at Houghton Toffee Works, Houghton-le-Spring, County Durham.

string-tailed sugar mouse, sold at four for a penny. Sweet, soft fondant proved a perfect filling for chocolate. Fry's of Bristol exploited this in Chocolate Cream Bars, first sold in 1866, and popular ever since.

Other soft, grained sweets developed. Coconut, imported in increasingly large amounts from the East, was transformed into pink and white layers of coconut ice. Fudge, home-made from milk, sugar and chocolate, was a particular favourite of North American students in the late nineteenth century.

Seaside rock became popular in the 1890s. This was a development of confections such as Gibraltar Rock (perhaps the derivation of 'rock' in this context), and of the sticks described by Mayhew (see page 13). Slabs of sugar were built up in complex longitudinal patterns, and the multicoloured lump pulled by hand into thin strings. When cool, it was cut into short sticks with the name of the resort magically running their length, and sold as a souvenir. Credit for inventing seaside rock has gone to, amongst others, Ben Bullock of Halifax and 'Dynamite Dan' of Morecambe. More prosaically, the secret was probably known to a few confectioners who exploited it until E. Skuse published instructions in his *Complete Confectioner* in the last decade of the nineteenth century.

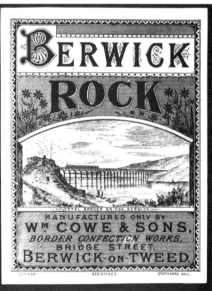

The river Tweed at Berwick illustrated on a late Victorian tin from Wm. Cowe & Sons. Now best known for striped, pulled 'Berwick Cockles', the company dates back to about 1800.

17

A village shop in 1885. For over a century, up to the Second World War, such little village stores provided sweets for most of the rural population.

Mass production

Describing a village sweet shop around the First World War, Christopher Ketteridge and Spike Mays (*Five Miles From Bunkum*, 1972) recalled how '"Fry's Cocoa" in faded capitals glared from one side of the window ... The counter bristled with glass jars of boiled sweets, black jacks, humbugs, pear-drops, aniseed balls, raspberry drops, acid drops, pepper-mints and chlorodyne lozenges.' Jars of boiled sugar continued to catch the eyes of youngsters, but advertisements for Fry's, which plastered shops all over Britain by the end of Victoria's reign, meant change was to come.

By 1880 chocolate sweetmeats made by Fry's, Cadbury's, Rowntree's and others were serious competition for sugar confectionery. Chocolate manufacture is quite different from sugar boiling, but its marketing, using bright wrappers and aggressive advertising, affected all sweets. Sugar confectioners, especially those making toffee, began to follow this trend.

Toffee received a boost in the 1880s when *caramels*, a North American innovation, were introduced. Caramels relied on slowly boiled sugar and milk to give a delicious flavour. Skuse wrote that these sweets were 'sold very freely in the lowest and poorest quarters of London, at two-pence per ounce; in the West End the same goods fetch double that price.' They were also suitable for mass production. Coco-nut oil substitutes were developed to replace the dairy products, and automatic stirrers replaced human endeavour at the boiling pan.

Confectioners began experimenting. In 1890 John Mackintosh opened a shop in Halifax. Shortly afterwards, he created Mackintosh's Celebrated Toffee, drawing

Pouring toffee at Welcher's toffee factory, Whitley Bay, Northumberland. Although this picture was taken in 1988, it shows a process unchanged for almost a century.

both on English toffee and American caramel formulae. In Maidstone, grocer Edward Sharp began to exploit family confectionery recipes. Sharp's became one of the best-known toffee companies; Kreemy toffee, developed in 1910, was followed in 1912 by Supreem and in 1923 by Superkreem. Other toffee companies from this time included Walters, Harvino (founded by Harry Vincent, near Birmingham), Walker Nonsuch (in Staffordshire) and Horner's (in Chester-le-Street).

Fruit sweets became more diverse. Chewy gums were not a new idea, but their quality had been uncertain. In 1830 Gunter had described gum jujubes as 'a sweetish sort of India-rubber'. Finemore had instructed how to boil calves' pates (skin from the heads) into strong jellied stock that was clarified, sweetened and coloured for 'shiver and shakey', yellow and red jelly set in layers.

In 1879 Rowntree's decided to manufacture high-quality pastilles and gums. A

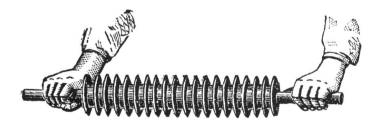

As they cooled, 'pourings' of toffee or caramels were cut with adjustable rollers such as these.

19

Boiling pans, probably containing sugar syrup, at Rowntree's in the late nineteenth century.

French confectioner, Claude Gaget (the French were leaders in this field), took charge, and in 1881 Rowntree's Fruit Pastilles were introduced. Twelve years later Rowntree's Fruit Gums joined them. Also of Victorian origin are Jelly Babies. As *Unclaimed Babies*, these are said to have been developed by an Austrian confectioner working for Fryer's of Lancashire in the 1860s.

Industrialisation in confectionery had begun slowly around 1830, when confectioners began measuring sugar concentration with a *sacharrometer*. Sugar boiling using 'degrees by thermometer' and cutting boiled sugar with a machine (probably drop rollers) was noted by Finemore by about 1840.

Craven's Clear Gums, a competitor for Rowntree's, in a 1925 presentation.

20

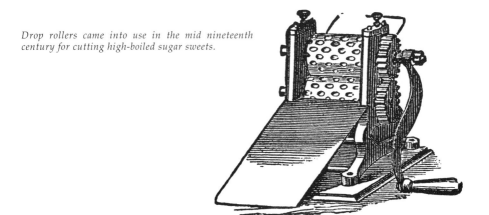

Drop rollers came into use in the mid nineteenth century for cutting high-boiled sugar sweets.

His manuscript shows confectioners working on a relatively large scale: 2 cwt (102 kg) of sugar a day was clarified. Boiling rooms must have been unsavoury places, where syrup generated clouds of steam, and bags, tacky with the residues of clarification, piled up. As with work in all industries, long hours in poor conditions were general, only improving towards the end of Victoria's reign. The pace of mechanisation increased rapidly round about 1880 in many confectionery departments, including lozenges and fondant production. The introduction of vacuum pans for high boilings (hard boiled sweets such as fruit drops) eased technical problems associated with mass production.

Cutting striped sweets at Joseph Dobson & Sons, Elland, West Yorkshire. Boiled sugar, still hot, is run through drop rollers, which stamp it with the pattern. Individual sweets are broken from the sheet when the sugar cools.

Liquorice, originally medicinal, expanded into an industry producing strips and sticks and spirals. Pontefract, already famous for chewy black 'Pomfret' cakes, became an important centre, with eleven companies working there in 1900. Local juice made by macerating liquorice roots was supplemented with dried 'block juice' from Spain (liquorice generally is called 'Spanish' in Yorkshire dialect) and root from the Levant. Liquorice sheets were layered with soft sugar paste, and Allsorts are said to have been accidentally mixed when a sample case of Bassett's lines was knocked over in 1899.

In North America industrialists were looking for a use for *chicle*, an opaque, elastic latex from Mexico. It had proved unsuitable for bicycle tyres. A tradition of chewing gum from

A 1925 advertisement for Wilkinson's of Pontefract. Liquorice was still grown near the town at this time.

22

The 'Confectioner's Handbook' (later Skuse's 'Complete Confectioner') was an important late-nineteenth-century work. The third edition shows the author leaning on a revolving comfit pan of the type that replaced the balancing pan, holding a sugar thermometer.

spruce trees suggested an idea. By 1890 several chewing gum companies were established, including Adams and Beech-Nut. In 1892 a young salesman, William Wrigley, began selling gum in Chicago. He was dynamic and innovative; Juicy Fruit was formulated in 1893 and Spearmint Gum in 1894. In 1911 Wrigley's Chewing Gum was introduced to Britain.

Companies exploited boiled sugar according to fashion. Callard & Bowser began making butterscotch and 'dessert nougat'. Barker & Dobson increased their range to include Everton Mints, Chocolate Eclairs and Buttered Brazils. Craven's French Almonds (sugared almonds perfumed with musk) were introduced in 1903. Pascall's extended operations to barley sugar, sugar sticks and almond rock. The Boer War had little effect on the confectionery industry beyond a rash of patriotic names such as Transvaal Toffee. Events such as Queen Victoria's Diamond Jubilee and Edward VII's coronation also provided marketing opportunities.

A company that eventually became a giant of British sugar confectionery was founded in 1906 when sugar boiler William Woodcock, grocer Robert Robertson, Sydney Marks and Thomas King each put £100 into a partnership. Robertson & Woodcock Ltd acquired Trebor House in Upton Park, London. The name 'Trebor' appealed to Robertson, who realised that if the letters were reversed it spelt 'Robert', and in 1921 Robertson & Woodcock became the Trebor Confectionery Company.

Between the wars: the corner shop

During the First World War sugar was scarce. Eventually it was rationed. Except for some residual guilt, campaigns to dissuade the public from the frivolous pastime of sweet-eating had little long-term effect on the national sweet tooth. One item that became more popular as a result of the war was chewing gum, as supplied to troops from the USA fighting in Europe. Bubblegum, based on a more elastic latex, followed in the 1930s.

Trade continued much as before. In a list now remarkable for the absence of brand names, Don Haworth (*Bright Morning*, 1990) described a corner shop in the 1930s:

> It was difficult not to dither, we were so spoiled for choice. There were hundreds of bottles full of strong-tasting sweets – mint imperials, gob-stoppers, aniseed balls, fruit gums, clear mints, lemon drops, pear drops, lime and sarsaparilla tablets. Then there were trays of toffee which had to be broken with a little hammer and which became so sticky on hot days that it could adhere permanently to a pocket lining. There were things parents did not like you to buy – chewing gum, braided spanish spooled round a coloured sweet and sticks of liquorice which left soft splinters of wood in your teeth.

CRISP AIR —
TAUT
NERVES

A keen game and a close one . . . nerves are strained, throats dry . . . Beech-Nut is throat cooling, nerve soothing. Its delightful flavour serves to sustain and heighten your enjoyment.

1 d.

Lasting and Refreshing

Beech-Nut
Chewing Sweets
THE CLEAN, COOL FLAVOUR OF MINT

Ranges made by numerous small firms broadly resembled each other. The 1919 merger of Cadbury's and Fry's foreshadowed rationalisation of the sugar confectionery industry after the Second World War.

In this crowded market, packaging and branding became increasingly important. In advertising, Sharp's led the way with their parrot trade mark and the catchphrase 'Sharp's Toffee speaks for itself'. In 1919 the character of Sir Kreemy Knut (probably modelled on Gilbert the Philbert, a character from a song) was launched on the front page of the *Daily Mail*. Rolls-Royces carried Sir Kreemy impersonators to holiday resorts. Other companies fought back with icons from popular culture. Child film star Jackie Coogan, Felix the Cat, Tiger Tim and

Chewing gum was popularised in Europe by North American troops during the First World War. Rowntree's of York acquired a controlling interest in Beech-Nut in 1928.

Mr Fish and his shop at Hetton-le-Hole near Durham. Selling fruit and confectionery together was quite usual in the nineteenth and early twentieth centuries.

Mickey Mouse all appeared on confectionery packaging. Dainty Dinah, a trade mark of Horner's, was the name of a waltz composed in 1925. Harry Vincent's company Harvino was renamed Blue Bird after the play *The Blue Bird of Happiness* in 1927.

Mackintosh's took a different approach. Whilst introducing new toffee lines (Toffee de Luxe in 1917 and Carnival Assortment in 1925), they began to concentrate on chocolate. In 1932 they acquired A. J. Caley & Sons, a Norwich company with a strong chocolate department. In 1936 a selection of toffees and chocolates was

Sharp's toffees were famous both for their flavour and for the verve with which they were advertised.

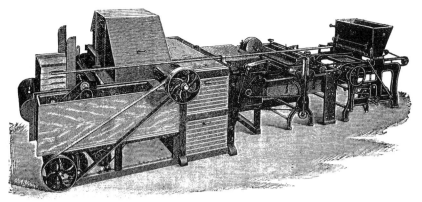

A mogul for industrial starch moulding. This automatically emptied trays, sieved the contents, re-filled them with starch, printed it, and filled the impressions. Fondants, gums, jellies and many other sweets are starch-moulded.

Above: *Starch line at Terry's York factory in the 1930s.*

Right: *Depositing fondant into impressions in a starch mogul at Terry's in the 1930s.*

introduced as 'Quality Street' (the title of a play by J. M. Barrie). Thornton's, founded in Sheffield in 1911, followed a similar route and Needler's also invested in a chocolate factory. This was a time of innovation for chocolate companies, when several classic brands were devised. Nevertheless, the filling for much chocolate was – and is – provided by sugar confectionery. Fry's Crunchie bars (launched 1929) are based on a confection similar to cinder toffee (boiled sugar aerated with bicarbonate of soda); Rolos (1937) contain caramel, and Smarties (also 1937) are made by panning.

Mint flavours had been popular for at least a century. Local products such as Jeddart Snails, Hawick Balls (both made in the Scottish borders), Uncle Joe's Mint

In the 1920s confectionery companies adopted motor transport. Some salesmen's vehicles were beautifully fitted out with mahogany drawers and cupboards containing samples of the sweets.

Balls (Lancashire) and the black bullets of north-eastern confectioners reflect these early sweets. Mint confections with higher profiles were now introduced. In 1909, Nuttall's of Doncaster began making minty, buttery 'Mintoes'. Fox's Glacier Mints, along with the polar bear trademark, were established nationally in 1920. Other branded mint sweets from this period include Barker & Dobson Creamy Mints, Trebor Mints, Clarnico Peppermint Creams and Bendick's Bittermints.

A fad for the oriental, apparent in the decorative arts, influenced confectionery. Coconut-flavoured candies with no obvious links to Japan were marketed as 'Jap nuggets'. Turkish Delight became popular (Fry's introduced their chocolate-covered version in 1914). Eastern influence gave the names *Phul-nana* and *Shem-el-nessim* to cachous made by Barker & Dobson. The use of sweets as breath-fresheners was given a boost by the production of ionone, a synthetic violet perfume. Wallflower, lily of the valley, lilac and other flower scents soon followed.

Children loved sherbet, also known as *kali* (the alkali bicarbonate of soda is an ingredient). As Rainbow Crystals, it recalled the bottles of ornamental sugar sands used by Georgian confectioners. Youngsters ate sherbet as dabs, dipping lollies into the powder. Doctors debated whether sherbet – intended as a mix

Jars used by Craven's for cachous (silver balls) flavoured with musk, floral essences or opopanax (a perfumed resin).

27

Above: *Revolving pans for making comfits at M. A. Craven, York, c.1935. This type of pan, still used, was the replacement for the now obsolete balancing pan.*

Left: *A childhood favourite since the late nineteenth century, sherbet, or kali, was sold in triangular paper bags with a lolly for 'dipping'. This packet, used by Maxilin Ltd, Bolton, commemorates the coronation of Queen Elizabeth II.*

for lemonade – could be harmful to children with delicate constitutions when eaten as powder. Confectioners seized on the link, and packaged sherbet in 'fountains' with liquorice straws.

Wrapping machines had been in use since the 1890s, but new ideas and materials (such as cellophane) were being introduced. The introduction of compressed sweets, using dry mixes shaped under pressure, allowed sherbet to be used as an ingredient in Refreshers and Love Hearts. Roll-wrapping, developed early in the twentieth century, meant these fragile sweets could be transported and retailed without problems. The age of the pre-pack had arrived.

Cheap and colourful sweets were constantly re-inventing themselves in new forms. Panning produced rifle balls and seaside pebbles. Sugar bird's eggs and jelly beans, both soft panned sweets, developed when glucose was added to centres for panning. Sugar paste and liquorice were given clandestine appeal by moulding them into sweet cigarettes and tobacco pipes. Some lines proved more popular than others, and shopkeepers discovered that slow movers sold faster in sealed 'lucky bags'.

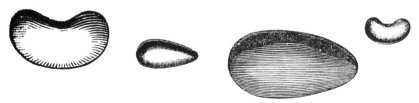

The use of glucose in sugar syrup allowed the development of soft panned goods. Shown here are patterns for making centres for jelly beans (a North American favourite) and sugar eggs.

Shortages of raw materials led to some confectionery being taken off the market during the Second World War. Advertising kept the memory of the product alive.

Rationing – and afterwards

During the Second World War imports of sugar, cacao and other ingredients were severely limited. Some factories (such as Trebor's in 1944) were bombed; others became munitions works. Part of the output was reserved for the forces, where many employees of confectionery factories now found themselves. Wrigley's, finding supplies of high-quality ingredients limited, took their gum off the market altogether and directed their entire output at US Armed Forces overseas. In Britain all sweets and chocolate were rationed by coupons from July 1942, a situation which lasted until February 1952 (with the exception of a few months in 1949). From an average consumption of 6 ounces (170 grams) of confectionery per head per week in 1939, consumers had to make do with 2 or 3 ounces (55-85 grams). Ice-cream production came to a halt.

Buying sweets and chocolate with coupons during the Second World War: three-quarters of a pound (about 350 grams) to last a month.

29

Processing sweets in Horner's sweet factory, Chester-le-Street, County Durham, in the 1950s.

A well-stocked sweet shop of the post-war period. Boxes, tins and 5 pound (2.23 kg) glass jars of branded confectionery have replaced the elegant tall jars of earlier decades.

Bertie Basset marches on. This sequence from the 1920s to the 1980s shows how sweets change and yet stay the same.

Sweets, like other items, were zoned for efficient distribution. This meant that brand names lost much of their power as they were limited to certain areas. Much ingenuity was exercised to use unconventional ingredients. When hostilities ceased in 1945 confectionery companies relied heavily on exports. They also looked forward to a brave new world; traditional recipes were out of fashion. What they wanted were innovators and technical wizards. But all confectionery is a gloss of fashion on old ideas. Mars' Spangles (1948) were recognisable as boiled sweets, just as Rowntree's Polo mints (also 1948) had their roots in a long sugar-paste tradition. Fun returned to confectionery in the 1950s as restrictions eased and were finally lifted in time for the coronation of Elizabeth II in the summer of 1953.

In the mid 1950s the first advertisement for sweets appeared on the new commercial television channels under the slogan 'Murray Mints, the too good to hurry mints'. It was about this time that consumption of sugar confectionery peaked in Britain. After this, the balance swung slowly in favour of chocolate and towards large companies. The industry was rationalised as small companies were gradually subsumed into larger ones. The colourful tradition of the small sugar confectioner, glimpsed across the counter in his backroom workshop, finally vanished behind the closed doors of factories.

Further reading

Brown, Peter, and Day, Ivan. *The Pleasures of the Table*. York Civic Trust, 1997. (Information about the development of the dessert course up to *c*.1820.)

Cakebread, Sidney. *Sugar and Chocolate Confectionery*. Oxford University Press, 1975. (A simple overview of the manufacture of sugar confectionery in the late twentieth century.)

Hendrickson, Robert. *The Great American Chewing Gum Book*. Chilton Book Company (Radnor, Pennsylvania), 1976.

Lees, Ron. *A History of Sweet and Chocolate Manufacture*. Specialised Publications (Surbiton), 1988.

Mason, Laura. *Sugar Plums and Sherbet: the Prehistory of Sweets*. Prospect Books (Totnes), 1998. (Sugar confectionery *c*.1500 – *c*.1900.)

Needler, Raymond. *Needlers of Hull*. Hutton Press (Beverley), 1993.

Opie, Robert. *Sweet Memories*. Pavilion Books, 1988; paperback edition, 1999.

Race, Margaret. *The Story of Blackpool Rock*. Blackpool, 1990.

Whittaker, Nicholas. *Sweet Talk: the Secret History of Confectionery*. Victor Gollancz, 1998. (The marketing of sugar confectionery in the twentieth century.)

Wilson, C. Anne. *'Banquetting Stuffe'*. Edinburgh University Press, 1991. (The evolution of the sugar banquet in the sixteenth and seventeenth centuries.)

Places to visit

Beamish, The North of England Open Air Museum, Beamish, County Durham DH9 0RG. Telephone: 01207 231811. Website: www.merlins.demon.co.uk/beamish (Early twentieth-century confectioner's shop and boiling room, with sugar-boiling demonstrations.)

John Bull Confectioners Ltd, Lancaster Road, Carnaby Industrial Estate, Carnaby, Bridlington, East Yorkshire YO15 3QY. Telephone: 01262 678525. Website: www.john-bull-confectioners.co.uk (Viewing gallery in factory; opening hours depend on season.)

Joseph Dobson & Sons, 26 Northgate, Elland, West Yorkshire HX5 0RU. Telephone: 01422 372165. (Factory tours and demonstrations for groups by appointment.)

The Museum of Advertising and Packaging, Albert Warehouse, Gloucester Docks, Gloucester GL1 2EH. Telephone: 01452 302309. (The Robert Opie Collection includes a large amount of material relating to confectionery.)

Rock Candy Kingdom, 415–417 South Promenade, Blackpool, Lancashire FY1 6BQ. Telephone: 01253 342257. (Demonstrations of rock-making; opening hours depend on season. Also at their Chapel Street shop, telephone: 01253 751136.)

Shaws Dundee Sweet Factory Ltd, Keiller Buildings, 34 Mains Loan, Dundee DD4 7BT. Telephone: 01382 461435. (Demonstrations of sweet-making; opening hours depend on season.)

York Castle Museum, Eye of York, York YO1 9RY. Telephone: 01904 613161. Website: www.york.gov.uk (Terry's confectioner's shop in Princess Mary Court; mid-nineteenth-century artefacts.)